Open book

Tessy Braun

Preface

Within this book you will discover a collection of open and honest poetry. The writing that you will find inside is real, raw and emotional, covering an assortment of topics such as depression, anxiety, heartbreak and parenting.

This volume of poetry is quite literally an *Open book* of my own life experiences, old and new. In addition there are a number of poems which are based on imagination and my love of storytelling. I truly hope that you can draw strength and inspiration from my words, and that you enjoy reading my poetry.

Love and light

Tessy x

Contents

Acknowledgments

I would like to thank my poetic friend Billy Harrington (**@thepoetbillyharrington** on Instagram) for being 'my rock' and supporting me through a number of difficult times over the last few years.

I'd also like to pay gratitude to the exceptionally supportive Instagram poetry community. I've made many like-minded friends across the globe, and being part of the community continues to be an extremely positive experience.

Finally, thank you to David for showing me that it *is* possible to be in a healthy, caring and happy relationship.

Honey

Poetry inspired by sweet and sour matters of the heart

Tessy Braun

Call to Prayer

Every morning we awoke
To the melodic *'call to prayer'*.

It was somewhat soothing
As those dulcet tones
Were carried through the air.

We lay together in anticipation
Of exploring the East,
And bathing in the sunshine
In the sticky Emirate heat.

I ran my hands over your shoulders,
Across your warm soft chest.
Embracing a moment together,
(Not once missing life in the West).

Complete

I feel **complete** with you!
You throw me into a dream land
Every time you take my hand
And pull my body close to yours,
Taking me away to paradise shores.

Everywhere tingles
And feels electric.
Stress drifts away,
And I'm no longer hectic.

I feel **complete** with you
When I'm sharing your heat
And kissing your mouth
And feeling you breathe.
I never want to leave.

In your strong embrace
Wrapped up, and delicately
Tangled together is somewhere
I want to be forever.

In your arms feeling so protected,
Wanted and precious.
Feeling so fiercely,
You leave me quite breathless.

I want to make you feel
Like no one has before.
Tingling, butterflies, buzzing,
And full of sweet amour!

**A piece I wrote circa 2007, which is a stark
reminder of how impermanent love can be!**

Modern Love

He loves me, he loves me not...
Before long I'll be forgot!
Because when push, comes to shove,
There's no staying in *'modern love'*.

Tessy Braun

Explore

Perfectly positioned,
My hand on your chest.
With you stroking my thigh,
The way I love best.

The TV is hushed,
The hours rush by,
My cheeks are flushed
And I'm feeling quite high!

It's now passed one a.m,
And I wish I could stay
Wrapped up in your arms
Until the next day.

Yet I have to insist
That you take yourself home
But you're hard to resist,
And I still want to roam!

Exploring your shoulders,
Your skin and your shape,
You're sexy and gorgeous,
But I know I must wait!

Unrequited

Once we were a couple so delighted.
Now we're just a love *unrequited*.

I always loved you more,
Than you ever liked me.

Despite this, I'm glad
We have our history...

(*Even though it wasn't meant to be*).

Tessy Braun

Catastrophe

Catastrophe, you and me.
Not a chance, don't you see?
For what I crave is *consistency*,
(An objective to live blissfully).

But you and me, we can't be right,
All we seem to do is fight.
We try and try with all our might,
Yet happiness is out of sight.

Lamb and Flag

Whenever I pass the *Lamb and Flag*,
On the A30 en-route to Penzance,
I think about you, as I give it a glance,
And remember well, our hot-headed romance.

And how we both adored the Cornish life,
And how you promised I would be your wife.
Though discord, just like the roaring sea
Washed our sandy love into our history.

Battered by waves crashing the rocks,
Corroded by the ocean that never would stop.
Yet I still remain fond of a time long forgot,
And I miss you sometimes, and still love you somewhat.

Tessy Braun

Happy Birthday

Say 'hello' to your forties,
Your best decade yet!
About to make memories
You will not forget!
I just cannot wait
Till we take to the sky
Across Europe and Asia
Destination Dubai!

You've my heart and my mind,
Tucked up in a box
In a puzzle to say
I care for you lots.
Happy birthday Mr Kempthorne
Of Cornish descent,
With love from your pixie
To my magical gent!

Communication

The missing key's *communication*

For any successful relation.
Compromise - the true foundation,
A level headed conversation.

Why whenever things get tricky
Must you get cross so very quickly?

You're the king of confrontation,
I watch you pour out your frustration,
You know it leads to devastation
And a self-loathing sensation,
To a pitiful destination
And ultimate alienation.

I just want to talk to you.
Is that such an unreasonable thing to do?
Try to stabilise your emotion,
It only causes a commotion,
Now the whole thing's cracked and broken
Just because I have spoken.

Tessy Braun

A Zillion Pieces

Is it better to leave now,
While I still have my mind?
Or to mend the cracks
And hope the glue will bind?
Is it possible to leave any
Sense of fragility behind?
Can we ever be strong again in time?

Or are we destined to shatter
Into a *zillion pieces*,

The same old tricks and somersaults.
Perhaps despite best intentions
It's time to finally **stop**.
But it feels *so* good,
Like sugar, sweet and hot...
But how long will that last
Before the happy times are lost?

Falling

I feel like a rainbow of
Butterflies are fluttering
All over my body.
Kissing me with their tiny wings,
Filling my life with colour
Happiness and heat.

I'm *falling* fast into a deep
Pool of purple passion,
It's swallowing me whole
And it tastes so sweet.

My feet are on the ground
But feel like they're in the sky.
My mouth tastes hot treacle
Sponge with custard
And zingy key lime pie.

It's all so delicious, we just can't get enough,
And if loving is food we're so nicely full up.
But are we *falling* in love, or is it just lust?

Tessy Braun

Little Child

Oh Lord, take me back to a time
When I felt loved and not despised.
Before fire and hate took lead
I felt a good thing was happening to me.
For once in my life this felt so right,
My dreams of happiness were in sight.

Something wonderful was about to start,
I would never have thought
You'd break my heart.

Warmth, desire, burning fire
Turned to hatred then expired.
Now I have this *little child*

Made from two hearts
That were once wild.

I'm not clear where the future lies,
Please God, send away the lows
And bring back the highs.

Four Strings

We met over *four strings*
Strung A to C.
Gorgeously shining maple
One instrument of destiny.

Your fingers traced the edge
Crushed from the drop.
You fixed my Cello with your hands,
My craftsman from the music shop.

Tessy Braun

Wild Place

A picnic in the meadow
With the grass turning yellow
The sun is hot and burning
And my heart is sweetly yearning.

A wild time among the cries
Of wolves echo through the skies.
Sandwiches, jelly and fruit we eat,
Poppadum crisps are up your street.

The cheetah's hidden in the shade,
The geladas too, I am afraid.
Yet talk of space and human race,
Makes a perfect day at this *wild place.*

Two Moon Sisters

Two moon sisters gazing into space,
Three thousand miles apart.
One's getting ready to go to sleep
The other ones day will soon start.

Celestial sisters gazing at the moon,
An ocean divided those fae.
Yet a moment so magical under the stars
Would conjure that ocean away.

Interwoven by the cosmos above
Despite the distance between,
It would take a day to reach by plane,
Though mere seconds through moonbeam.

Two lunar sisters with eyes upon the moon.
Betwixt them an ocean that gleams
One about to close her sleepy eyes
And the other just awoke from her dreams.

.

Tessy Braun

Crush

I've always had a *crush* on you,

I wonder if you guessed?
Would it surprise you very much
That I fancied you the best?

Oh what a fury we'd have caused,
The ultimate shock betrayal,
Breaking unpenned friendship rules,
So over lustful thoughts I must prevail!

Already Taken

Hypnotising, electrifying and satisfying.
My admiration for him is rapidly intensifying!
He's so engaging, smart, funny and kind
(The kind of man that's hard to find).

And although I'm searching
For the one that will be mine,
This adorable man must be forsaken
Because a wedding ring tells me
He's *already taken*!

I'll Be Here

Take my hand, I'll help you through
The times when you are feeling blue.
On days you don't know what to do,
I'll try my best to comfort you.

> For even though we're not the same
> And won't accept each other's blame,
> Despite not sweet like sugar cane
> *I'll be here* should you call again.

Passion

Tonight we went to the Ordolph,
Then we went to The Cornish.
Rob is cool, Chris's mate,
Then Chris I started to hate.

But when we got back,
Passion, Passion

I told him I was pissed off,
He told me I was beautiful.

This is a poem that was written when I was a teenager. One of many, among a multitude of handwritten poetry in various journals and diaries. My love of writing started at a very young age, and it is interesting to read diaries from the viewpoint of my nine year old self!

Tessy Braun

The Perfect Look

The perfect look into his mind,
Gazing in those perfect eyes.
The way when we're both
Holding tight,
Feels so right.

His hands so perfect,
masculine,
So warm, inviting,
So real, so vivid.

Ears that would listen,
Hear forever,
Soft sweet and small,
Room for all.

Belly with such dark hairs,
Looks so sexy in jean flairs.
Body so muscular,
Everything I want, he's got!

Teeth so bright and determined,
Voice so tender and rough.
Enough to melt me.

This poem was written when I was a teenager and it is about my first boyfriend. Chris was a member of a band called "Hat Stand" and I used to adore watching him sing and play his guitar.

First Date

She glanced at her watch,
Nearly time for her *date*.

Excited and nervous,
She just couldn't wait.

She strode up the mall,
With confidence portrayed,
When she spotted the man
She was by no means dismayed.

Devouring a cake slice,
It was delectably nice,
Gorgeously melty
Just like the man's eyes!

He was sexy and clever,
Witty and fun,
But her mind kept on dreaming
About his cute bum!

The chatter flowed
With plentiful charm,
And she knew from that moment
He would cause her no harm.

I See You

I see you, Hotshot guy,
Suave and sexy behind your desk.
My thoughts do wander from my list
Of things to do, so I'll tell you this.

> I must confess, I've liked you less,
> Before, when you've been unfair to Tess,
> But now I find you really hot
> And all that '*banter*' I forgot.

So meet me in the conference room,
Be sure to bring the key.
I'll show you what I think of you,
And you can make it up to me...

This is the first of a series of four "racy" poems that I created out of pure imagination. I really enjoyed writing these pieces. They were fun and really took my mind of the more serious things that were going on in life at the time. They're supposed to be cheeky, and a bit of light relief. I hope you enjoy them but if racy is not your cup of tea you may want to skip to page 35!

You See Me

You see me,
You caught my eye.
Read my email, don't be shy.
You ping me back.
"Tess, what time?",
I message back "Half past nine".

I'm there first, face to the glass,
Your hand slides down across my back.
You take my shoulders, spin me round,
Whisper me the sweetest sounds.
You step away to close the blind,
Some privacy we hope to find.

You pin me up against the wall,
And oh my God, I start to fall
Into your arms, into your mouth,
And then you start to wander south.

We don't resist each other's touch
(Though I never liked you all that much).
Then buttons start to come undone,
Now you're Tess's No.1,
Think it's time to have some fun.

Softly, gently you come in,
Make me fizz and whirl within.
Beating hearts, hot and flushed,
Don't you think this feeling's lush?
Got a sense this date's been rushed.

Ooh Hotshot guy, it's ten o-clock,
And on the door we hear a knock!

Tessy Braun

Lunch Hour

Hotshot guy, did we go too far
When you took me for a drive by car?
The best *lunch hour* I've had by far,

Yet circumstances seem bizarre.

Pulled up right outside my home
You say you want me all alone.
Turn the key and in you're shown,
Kick off your shoes, turn off your phone.

I peel off my office wear
And then let down my tied up hair.
Pull the curtains, dim the lights,
Then reveal my crotchless tights!

You try to touch, I push you down,
Can't help but giggle when you frown.
I sit myself upon the chair,
Spread my legs and touch down there.

Your mind and body can't resist,
And all you want to do is kiss.
(I still can't believe we're doing this!).
The fun and games are fucking bliss.

Now we must go back to work but
Before we do, you turn me 'round,
Tap my bum and bend me down,
Admire my figure, you're so aroused.

I'm resisting any sexual acts,
But you sure have an itch to scratch.
I watch you do what you must do,
A *lunch hour* to remember for me and you!

Crave

I still **crave** for your tongue,

And for your shirt to come undone.
God, I've missed you so darn much,
I'm sat here longing for your touch.

> You always gave me that 'melty' feel,
> The one that made your loving real.
> And I liked when you were rough,
> I could never get enough.

Tessy Braun

Time Heals

They say *time heals*,

Well isn't that true,
There's hardly a day
When I still think of you.

I can barely recall
A time when I cared,
My memory is fading,
No longer impaired.

Once I felt anger,
Now there's no hate.
Perhaps I feel pity
For my dear old *'mate'*.

I see you're still loathing
And can't let things drop,
But to me you are nothing
Your existence *forgot*.

A Man's Touch

I'm strong, but I miss a *man's touch*,
I need some comfort and want to lust.
To feel his hand stroke my head,
Tangled up together in my bed.

To sleep upon a man's soft chest,
I'm craving this I must confess.
Though I'd be the first to suggest,
Who needs a man, being single is best!

Yet maybe it's all catching up with me!
Perhaps I'm fed up of living independently?
A man to kiss away the tears that fall,
To be intimate, deep and sensual.

Maybe this is all the meds I need?
Some loving please Doc, perhaps indeed,
So I'll be willing to take the dose,
The kind of meds I need the most...

Tessy Braun

Being Single Rocks

I know I always tend to moan,
But *actually* I quite like being on my own!
I've got fantastic friends
And magnificent mates,
There's just no point going on dates!

Come on girls, who needs a guy
When you've got a friend?
A boyfriend will only
Drive you 'round the bend.
Yes, maybe it's exciting and
Sure fun at the start,
But he'll more than likely
Break your heart!

Or worse...

He'll keep you up all night
With that dreadful snore,
Or you'll be constantly nagging him
To close the bedroom door.
And he'll make such a mess!
And even though he will try his best
(Yet only in vain).
You'll never have a tidy house again!

No, romance can be put on hold,
Maybe someday
Something special may unfold,
But for now, as the clock tick tocks,
Being single really ROCKS!

Carefully

Her heart, light and giddy
Like feathers.
Yet her conscience dark
And heavy like lead.
She said "Never get lost
In these dreams of forevers,
So *carefully, carefully* I must tread".

Tessy Braun

Quiz Me, Test Me

A shady spot beneath the trees,
Sipping shake, just you and me.
Denim blue and gorgeous you
Lying on my side to enjoy the view.

Quiz me, test me, you may undress me,

Your nerdy brain does impress me.
Chatting, chilling and if your willing,
Lean over, kiss me, temptation's killing.

Shake's finished, time's diminished,
It flew away, I cannot stay.
Imagination isn't wasting,
I fancy you there's no mistaking!

I Adored You

I adored you, but why?
What was the sickly purpose
For you to come in to my life?
You were new, I had hopes for us,
But did I think they'd turn to dust?

Maybe, maybe I had doubts,
But I only wanted to know your where-abouts.
What was so wrong to want to know,
Or to be shown
Where you sleep and where you keep?

A summer of sweet memories,
A summer of sweet loving.
It just meant *nothing*!
A waste of breath lying softly on your chest,
(Where I liked to be best).

Take a deep breath in,
Block it all out.
Shut it away,
Don't think of a single day.
I adored you, but why?

Tessy Braun

Love Fairy

Sat by the sea
Carefully fishing
For something that
I 'think' I'm missing.

Clicking
Scrolling
Browsing
Spying

Oh the prospect is so exciting,
Eagerly searching for something inviting!

Smiling
Chatting
Coffee
Dinner

I think I may be onto a winner,
But chit-chat doesn't flow the same,
And interest then does not sustain,
So time to start the game again.

Clicking
Scrolling
Browsing
Spying

But now in truth I feel like crying!
Will I ever meet my perfect date?
Or would *'Love Fairy'* have me wait?

For All The Heartache

For all the *heartache* we've been through

For all the hurtful things you do
For all those unkind statements too,
I'm telling you now, how much I love you.

For all the nasty things I've said,
For all the messing with my head,
And for all the anger that we fed,
For all the salty tears we shed

I'm telling you now, how much I love you

Tessy Braun

Want

I *want* to fall into your depth,

Savouring each addictive breath.
I crave escape right into you,
There's nothing else I want to do.

When I'm swimming in your lust,
For a fleeting time I just
Forget about my wavering world,
When you shower me in gold and pearls.

I want to sink right into you,
There's nothing that I wouldn't do
To feel your heat and heavy breath,
I want to sink into your depth.

Author Day

Author day starts with a nice cup of tea,
Then we eat up our croissants **de**liciously!
You at your laptop and me and mine,
Author day - six blissful hours of rhyme!

Quietly crafting wandering words,
Facing each other trying not to disturb,
Though every so often a chatter and chirp,
With pixie ears on, we attentively work!

Lunchtime arrives and now time for our soup,
(Tomato and garlic – it tasted so good!).
And quickly you kindly pop out to the shop,
After realisation the cheese was forgot!

Profiteroles next, the dessert we adore!
Yet not quite satisfied and still room for more,
There's just enough time for one final treat –
We take pleasure in cuddles that pudding can't beat!

Back to our desks for the afternoon shift,
I try and focus on work but my mind is adrift,
Thinking of how much I wanted to stay,
So we're already planning the next author day!

Tessy Braun

Desert

If it should not last till the sun's setting glow,
If in the soft wind love gently blows,
And Middle East breezes
Sweep the *desert* sands adrift,

Your sweet kiss will always be missed.
Yet no matter what obstacle may arise,
I'm glad I fell into your eyes.
You've taken me up into the sky,
And inspired me to take that flight,
Above the clouds, above the city,
With those Emirate lights so pretty,
Into the dunes, the stars and moon.
But if it should not last till the suns setting glow,
I'm glad that I've known you,
And for the sunshine you've shown.

Open Book

Tessy Braun

Toxic

Poetry inspired by experiences of emotional and violent mistreatment.

Tessy Braun

Too Late

You left me so sick when I begged you stay.
Yet you left me for dead
(Can't get this out of my head).
It's *too late*.

> You grabbed my neck, then threw me down,
> Then you twisted my arm.
> (But it'll do me no harm and
> Should cause no alarm).
> *So you say.*

It's not okay! It's *too late!*

> You couldn't love the one I loved,
> Always on guard, always too hard.
> (I know it's a challenge, yet one I cannot discard).

It's really *too late.*

And although I appreciate your pain,
I can't see how anything would change,
So it's really, much better
We remain - estranged.

Tessy Braun

The Obsession

Returning to the pit of blame
For a bloody battle full of shame.
Although I still feel hot from the flame,
It burns me just the same.

While searching for something warm,
Instead I fell into a storm,
And now the rain is dragging me
Down, down, down.

Oh to start from a-fresh,
To love you once again,
I do so wish for the best,
And to be rid of all this blame.
To be forever happy and kind,
But you really must…
Leave '*The Obsession*' behind.

Leopards

If only love was enough to make
A person change their ways.
Sadly it's rarely the case these days.
And *leopards* tend not

To change their spots,
Whether they feel in love or not.

Tessy Braun

Rattle

Sneaky, manipulative and devious.
The world doesn't see, *but I do*.

You think I don't know how you operate,
The world doesn't see, *but I do*.

Professing love but causing conflict,
You think I don't realise, *but I do*.

I know, it's you, hiding behind the mask,
Hiding like a coward, *I see you*.

I Will Survive

Whatever you do,
Whatever you say,
You can't break me,
I'm here to stay.

Wherever you are,
However you try
To crack my soul,
I will survive.

Insignificant then,
Insignificant now,
Not worth a breath,
Not worth a row.

Just don't ever think
I won't say the truth,
If you step out of line,
I've got nothing to lose.

Tessy Braun

Lies

Lies seep through its teeth,
Like melted butter.
Running, dripping, oozing.

Its syrup not sweet,
Its taste foul and stale,
Fighting, calling, losing.

Its fingers reach out,
With words; tap, tap, tap.
Sorting, picking, choosing.

The Bear

May they all be aware
Of the big black *bear*

That pads in the woods,
Looking misunderstood.

He is not what he seems,
With his visions and dreams,
And his cuddly fur coat.
(For he'll soon cut your throat).

So please carefully tread,
Or you may wind up dead.
Do not get too near,
It will cost you my dear!

Though his honey attracts,
You know not the facts,
Dismiss his lame cries
When tears fall from his eyes.

Think twice 'fore you meet,
For his nectar's unsweet,
As it drips from his teeth,
And the poison's released.

May they all be aware
Of that big black *bear*

That pads in the woods
Looking misunderstood.

Tessy Braun

Lamb To The Slaughter

Like a *lamb to the slaughter*
I watch, but cannot save her skin.
She is dancing with delight
Towards a trap to draw her in.

Like a *lamb to the slaughter*

I want to shout and scream,
Don't get caught up in his net
For he is not what he seems.

Warn

We don't know each other,
But I need to *warn* you.

> I have tried,
> But I don't know if you got the hint.

I am itching to shout and scream
Girl! He is not what he seems!

> You may be too young and fresh
> To smell a rat but

I knew from very early on
And then, it really wasn't long

> Before I found out I was not the only one
> (Among all the 'so called' fun)

To get caught up in his trap
But wise to his type, I did not do that.

> So please tread carefully beauty,
> The beast is closer than you may imagine.

Tessy Braun

Each Bird

Each little *bird* that flaps around his jaws
Is naïve to how he treats his whores.
There's no sweet taste, only bitterness drips
From the poison that his mouth emits.

Friend Or Foe?

We're the good guys,
Whom you can trust.
We're your friends,
You can rely on us!

(That's what you hear
As they suck you in
With promise of love,
From the Chief Kingpin).

Yet can you be sure,
Are they *friend or foe*?
Better watch your back,
'Cuz you never really know...

Tessy Braun

For None Would Hear
(Excerpt)

He said he had a nice surprise
While his family wait inside,
Envisioning a sweet display
On this grim and gruesome day.

He produced a scarf and held her chin,
"My sweet, before we both go in,
I want to take a moment here",
He kissed her lips and drew her near.

Then before she could surmise,
He secured the scarf around her eyes.
Lead her to a run-down hut,
Tied her hands, began to touch.

She did at first enjoy the fun,
(Where buttons had become undone).
But touches were not so gentle as
They had been given in the past.

Sensing things were getting strange
His actions then became deranged.
She pleaded him to stop the game,
Yet he carried on just the same.

Grabbing, pulling, punching, biting,
Wasn't long 'fore they were fighting.
She did not want him touching so,
She screamed for him to let her go...

This is an excerpt of a narrative poem which explores the tragic consequences of domestic abuse. The full piece can be purchased on Amazon Kindle.

Sly Fox

You *sly fox*,
Cunning and mean.
I know that your life
Is not what it seems.

You lied about this,
You lied about that.
You are one despicable
Deceitful old twat!

Tessy Braun

Fool

What is this repugnant familiar stench,
That seeps through your sticky web of pretense?
Your language and manner is one of disgust,
Not one rancid word should any one trust!
It's sickening right to my stomach and core,
That everyone thinks you're the hero and more.
Yet I know a fair few who would
Knock down your door,
Or throw a brick though your window
You pathetic old *fool*.

Wolf

Walking through the woods at dusk
A *wolf* attacked, and at me thrust.
A wicked *wolf* of the night,
He pounced on me and took a bite.

Tessy Braun

I Followed Her

I followed her this morning,
Tried calling out her name,
I longed for her to know
How he'd caused me so much pain.

Crying out my story,
In attempt to make her see
The fury of his temper
And his cruel brutality.

She never heard a word,
Maybe choosing to ignore.
I'm hoping she'll remember
When he throws her to the floor.

When he pulls her pretty hair
Or when he grabs her chin,
When he tells her she's no good,
Letting out his rage within.

I wish that I'd got through to her
With the warning that I gave,
I hope that she will leave him,
I hope that she'll be brave.

Oh God, for I wish I'd listened
To that desperate hopeless plea,
When my boyfriend's ex-lover
Once attempted to warn me.

So take heed from my message
Which to this vicious world I share,
For my broken heart and bruises,
Are now disastrously not there.

Penny

When will the **penny** drop?
When will the curtains close?
When will all these pretty girls
Wreck you with what they know?

When will the clapping cease?
When will your flock disperse?
When will your lies become exposed
Revealing your deceptive verse?

Parasite

He lives in his fantasy world,
'Make believe' his therapy of choice.
He clings to the belief of self-righteousness
Maintaining he has the superior voice.

This *parasite* always infecting,
Burying under your skin.
Your intuition I hope will guide you
To shut the door when he tries to come in.

Prey

I won't fall victim to your *prey*,
I'll have more sense and walk away.

> Don't blame me for what's occurred,
> It's your behavior that's absurd.

> Prey all you like, I see you hunt,
> You won't catch me you fucking cunt.

Tessy Braun

Icy Witch

How can the *Icy Witch* be so cruel?
This wicked witch emits no warmth at all.
How can she sleep with ease at night,
Her conscience weighing heavy on her mind.

How can the Savage Hex be so grim?
Showing no compassion deep within.
How can she cry through those pewter eyes,
When there's no love left to find inside?

The answer is so evidently clear,
You'll never catch her shed an honest tear.
Her heart of stone lodged firmly in her chest,
Insisting her vindictive ways are best.

Open Book

Tessy Braun

Mind

Poetry inspired by stress, anxiety and depression

Tessy Braun

What If?

Could someone please tip me upside down,
And shake me around fiercely?
Perhaps that would make the worry
Fall out of my head?

Maybe someone could punch me in the nose
And tell me I'm a *silly*, *silly* girl,
Maybe that would work instead?

It's alright! I've got this,
There's no way it's so!
Wait! *What if?*

I'll just look online,
Just one more time...

Oh shoot, I shouldn't have played that game,
Can someone shake me upside down again?

Wasted

This overwhelming panic
Trickles through my veins like poison.
Consuming me completely.
Rational thinking no longer exists,
My anxiety eats me up
From the inside out, so sweetly.

I've delved into rabbit holes,
Interrogating the web all night.
Obsessively clawing into
Each pocket and sleeve.
Perfecting my knowledge to be
Greater than any doctor may achieve.

So – much – time – wasted.

Want – this – worry – obliterated.

Without Doubt

Without doubt
Time's running out.
Half way to seventy,
Is growing old a necessity!?
Life's so full of complexity...

But it is *so* short,
And soon near the end you may be caught
Distraught, with one agonising thought...

Why did you waste away all your years,
Battling your anxiety and
Fighting back your tears?

A reflective, yet positive piece encouraging my readers to remember that we are not here for a long time, so please don't waste that time being sad and unhappy, you will only regret it.

Tessy Braun

Autumn Leaves

Fallen *Autumn leaves* leave me
Feeling a fraction better.
Yet I still carry a taste so bitter.
Chilling gusts of wind and sharp icy rain,
But nothing, just nothing will
Soak away this ugly stain
Of shame and blame.

Stress

Stress levels are rising high.

Stay calm Tess (I really try).
So I constrain and grit my teeth,
Tense my body up from my feet.
Count to ten and breathe in deep.
Walk away from burning heat
And my composure I will keep.

Tessy Braun

Set Me Free

Creativity *set me free*.
Break me away from the
Demon in me.

Each stroke of the brush,
Each word written down,
Each tender note played,
My escape is then made.

Trapped

Trapped in a gaol awaiting my fate,
Boiling in envy, inadequacy and hate.
What have I done to deserve such a hell,
Are childhood misdemeanors
My punishment still?

Trapped in a vessel,
Caught in a storm,
Curse that this mother was born!
Years have passed quickly,
I wish more would slide
Right though my fingers
And out of my mind.

Dreams turned to nightmares,
Objectives not met.
Hopes not fulfilled,
A life full of regret.

Out in the ocean, bobbing on waves,
Deep in a cliff face – lost in a cave.
Anywhere but here, I long to escape.

Tessy Braun

Lavish

When you look at me
In festival colours,
I display my feathers
With *lavish* endeavor.

Yet when the night falls
And the curtains close,
While the lonely wolf cries
Tears spill from my eyes.

Yuletide Blues

This is a *Yuletide* consumed by darkness,
Lost inside the unforgiving arctic
Of her depression,
Colourless and void

And if there's a hint of happiness
It's soon ferociously destroyed.

Tessy Braun

My Dear Friend

Clouds moving into my sky,
Dark shadows floating by.
Soon to engulf me, in my entirety,
Smother me whole,
My dear friend, Anxiety.

Medusa

Medusa with one fiery glance,

Transform me into stone.
For then all my heart ache,
Stress and grief is sure to go.

Medusa with your viper locks,

Solidify me with your stare,
Make my tears no longer run
With your hissing serpent hair.

Medusa let me in your cave,

I won't try to slay you dear.
Pierce my skin with deadly venom,
I'll look at you and have no fear.

Blank Canvas

No longer is my *canvas blank*,

In many ways sad to say.
My crisp 'white as snow' page
Has now turned a shade of grey.

There is no turning back.
What's done cannot be changed.
Sadly, moments lost in time
Cannot be rearranged!

I wrote this poem after the birth of my first son, and soon after the relationship with his father broke down. I contemplate that I will no longer ever have a fresh start with someone new because my page has already been written on, having had a child already.

Growing Older

When I was little I longed to grow old,
Pining for my future and what it would hold.
A husband, children and my very own home,
Life would be blissful, I'd not be alone.

Yet now I am **grown**, it's not how I predicted,
In a prison of sadness I've now been convicted.
Being grown-up is not how I foresaw,
With no such return to my life from before.

A treasured picture of my father and me in North Cornwall. I must have been about 5 years old. Our dog was called Tamsin. Happy days, if only we could return to childhood, I'd go back in a flash!

Tessy Braun

Losing all Hope

I'm feeling so stressed,
I can no longer cope,
There's jobs mounting up
And I'm *losing all hope*!

The house needs a blitz,
The garden needs work.
There's bills to pay,
I'm going berserk!

The kids never help,
They just make a mess.
I'm not pretty or prim,
Always feeling depressed.

I'm sobbing within,
Everything is a struggle.
No time for violin
And I'm feeling a muddle...

Can't keep up with letters,
Homework and reading.
Will it ever get better -
This miserable feeling?

Black Dog

The *black dog's* back.
Or whatever you'd like to call him.
The fog, the mist, the hell within,
The sadness, the desperation.
Condemned to damnation!

> The hopelessness, the tears,
> The panic and fears,
> Will the doom and gloom shake?
> Or is this my fate?

> Either way, I feel the pup
> Has jumped on me and ate me up.
> I ty to run, I try to swim,
> But I can't escape, I'll never win.

Tessy Braun

Love Thy Neighbour

The cow next door is raging

Her brats are fighting too.
She lets them run a riot,
She lets them run the roost!
They wake us up at six,
Running up and down the stairs,
She doesn't try to shut them up,
It's like she doesn't care!
She lacks all due respect,
She makes us all so stressed!
She's got some serious issues
That need to be addressed!
So I text her in the morning,
Ask if she intends to stay
Inside with screaming children
Not preventing rows all day.
I say that she allows it
And all the neighbours think the same.
I tell her it's *her* fault,
I make her feel like *she's* to blame.

What the neighbour doesn't realise

Is that behind the bedroom wall,
There's a mother weeping silently
Who can't cope anymore.
She's tried all the strategies,
She's tried for years and years,
But the awful daily meltdowns
Leave her in desperate tears.
She wants to crash the car,
Or drown in the bath,
A little empathy from thy neighbour,
Is that all too much to ask?

Sister, Sister

Sister, sister please don't worry.

We'll try to keep each other jolly.
We spend too much time
Feeling sad and glum,
About these things that will not likely come.

Please remember what will be will be,
For we can only act cautiously.
Stop worrying until you have no choice,
That's my new philosophy.

Sister, sister we'll not be broken,

So stay strong and help each other through.
We both have precious babes to love,
And don't forget that I love you too!

Tessy Braun

Mask

You say the pills are working
And you smile all day long!
(Yet still in your heart you know
Deep down your marriage is all wrong).

It's just the medication's working
You feel a buzz within,
There's less desire to smack his face
And patience doesn't wear so thin.

But is this the way to live your life,
To exist in pretense while *masking* the lies?

How long can you live this dishonest fashion,
In a romance empty of love and compassion?

State Of Mind

It never seems to rain, it pours,
Always stuck between the lion's jaws.
So close to hear its hungry raw
Destined bad luck forever more.

Or is this just a *state of mind*,
If the negative we always find?
Is destiny in your able hands?
Or is it choice or fate for every man?

Tessy Braun

If I Should Live

If I should live

Twelve years more,
I'm going to run faster
Than ever before.
I'm going to pack,
And set myself free
When I'm out of the prison
That suffocates me.
I'm going to drive
And not stop for a break,
To the ocean of dreams,
Then I'll make my escape.
It's going to be silent
But the roll of the waves
And with a pen in my hand
The most peaceful of days.

If I should live

If I should live

Halloumi

Sometimes
When I pick up a knife,
I imagine stabbing myself,
Repeatedly in the chest,
Because last night
I ate way too much
Halloumi

Tessy Braun

Nurture

Poetry inspired by the trials and tribulations of
parenting

Tessy Braun

Nine Years

I've clocked *nine years* of being mum,

Raising two spirited boys.
There's no denying it's hard as hell,
(But definitely very rewarding as well).

But even though I'm *nine years* in

I don't profess to hold within
The ever flowing font of knowledge
That makes you perfect and ever polished.

There are certain things I read or hear
And listen with an open ear,
But truthfully may not agree
And often think it's 'OTT'.
Yet remind myself it's not for me
To judge or comment recklessly.

We all have life experiences,
They make us who we are.
We may feel the need to guide,
Just don't take it all too far!

A family "Selfie" taken on a trip to LEGOLAND in celebration of Joshua's 5th birthday. There is no perfect mother, but I do try my best.

Tessy Braun

Happy Days

Life feels stressful, life seems tough.
Hopes and dreams may turn to dust,
But I try to remember this, *I must.*

These are my memories and **happy days**,
And sometime when I'm old and grey
And looking back at yesterday,
At these moments so far away -
Now only in my heart and mind,
Wishing they weren't left behind.

So when you're feeling hopelessly tired,
When happiness appears expired,
You must force yourself to think
That life is short and in a blink
You'll be longing these days to reappear,
So enjoy them while you can my dear.

One of my favourite photographs of me and my older son Oliver. Taken during a photoshoot at Ashton Court in Bristol, United Kingdom, 2015.

You Crazy Lot

I told him not to jump,
I told them both to stop!
Our house is not a circus,
Please behave *you crazy lot*!

No, please don't do a front flip,
One of you will slip!
Too late…!
(Front teeth pierced through his bottom lip).

Screams and panic start proceeding.
"Mummy! Tell me, is it bleeding?"
"Yes, now come here my little one
The circus show is now all done".

Tessy Braun

Summer

The *summer* churns to an end.

My little son off to school,
Even though he seems too small.

I can still hardly believe
That my big son will be ten next year.
Growing up fast, adolescence looms near.

I'll wipe it away with autumn breeze
And look forward to see what they'll learn.
Soon the holidays will come again,
So let's look ahead to the next half term!

Born

A new life *born* – a baby boy!
Mum's overwhelmed and full of joy!

She survived the trauma of childbirth.
(A reward which they *say* the pain **is** worth).

But now she's got to survive the rest,
And God only knows she tries her best...

In April 2008 Oliver was born after a long and traumatic birth. I felt overwhelmed with my new son. I loved this tiny boy from the moment I held him, but it wasn't an easy ride and still isn't today. However as I said in a poem a few pages back, these are my happy days and I should do well to remember that.

Tessy Braun

Sweet Sound

Listen to this *sweet sound* of nothing!

There's no little people to
Demand my attention,
And it feels so *awfully* good!

There's a long list of jobs to complete,
But with no interruptions
The process will be a breeze!

And hopefully, with a little bit of luck,
If I get on with it quickly enough,
They'll be time for a run, and to read.

But first, before the countdown
To chaos begins,
I think I'll enjoy one last cup of tea!

Enough

I've never known anything other
Than playing the role of the single mother,
And lately I've been feeling
That I've just had *enough*,
It's been exhausting and incredibly tough!

(Can I hand over to you
For the **next** one hundred and
Twenty one months!?)

Tessy Braun

Goddess

She writes like she is the oracle
Or the *goddess* of motherhood.

I so wish I could claim to be
Just a *fraction* as good.
But evidently I can never aspire to be
Anywhere even near to
Her maternal supremacy.

Best Job

It's known to be the *best job* ever
(Yet that's dependent on the weather).
And in our house it rains a lot,
So blue skies and sunshine are mostly forgot.

Crying and moaning,
Winging and groaning,
Growling and howling,
Shouting and scowling.

They say being a parent in the *best job* of all,

Yet most days I could throw
My fist through the wall,
And I don't feel very maternal at all!

Tessy Braun

Rainbow Hell

Claustrophobic *rainbow hell*,

Deafening tunes blare out as well.
Sticky fingers with germs a-flying,
Stuffy and mucky, there's no denying.

Coffee calls, perhaps cake too,
The children screech and barge right through.
Cries of delight with shrieks of distress
In a jungle of chaos, small people and mess.

Avoid the kids who cough my way,
The sweaty stench won't go away.
They jump for joy on a castle of air,
While I sip my coffee and wish I'm elsewhere.

Incessant Screaming

From morning to evening
I cannot escape,
This *incessant screaming*
Starts a soon as I wake.

This eternal cacophony,
I can't bear any more,
I shout out like a monster
And run for the door!

I run far from home
Until I'm alone,
Away from the screech
That never will cease!

Tessy Braun

My Little Whirlwind Boys

I honestly think my children may
Send me to an early grave.
Will there actually be a time
When they might consistently behave?

I try to be calm, I really do,
But sometimes the constant squealing
Really grates on you.

I am thankful though,
Because I love my babes,
And I am lucky to have them,
And there's nothing I would change!

Apart from...

If they could be
A little more calm
And less noisy?
If they could just
Get along a *little*
More nicely?
Am I asking too much?
Yes, less noise
Would certainly be appreciated
my little whirlwind boys!

Two Little Lines

The most agonising of decisions
Seem easy to make,
And *two little lines* are so easy to take.

Though you may still imagine
What may be at stake,
The fact still remains
It would be a mistake...

When I posted this poem on Instagram I asked for my readers' interpretation. No one understood the real meaning of "Two Little Lines". Some thought it was about drugs, some thought marriage vows, and others thought it represented an apology. No one was right. What do you think it is about?

Tessy Braun

Ficta

Poetry inspired by imagination and story telling

Tessy Braun

Suzanne

Gather around and I'll tell you a story I found
About *Suzanne*, a girl with a putrid plan.

She was upset so badly and always lived sadly
To have a chance to be happy
She had to *punish* her man!

One morning when he was asleep in his bed,
She quietly slipped on her shoes.
She went out the back door and into the shed,
Where she had hidden a machete
To cut off his head.
She sneaked back into the
Room and then onto the bed,
She straddled the man and did what I said.
After the deed she felt she were freed
From this awful life that she
Thought she did lead.

But, what had he done to deserve such a fate?
Was he unfaithful?
Why did murder await?
Did he pull her long hair
And treat her with hate?
Did he belittle her,
Shame her or reel her in with his bait?

No...

His crime was leaving his clothes on the floor,
For not closing the bathroom door,
For not wiping the sink,
For not cleaning away that drink.
For not hanging the wet clothes to dry,
For not dressing smartly with a suit and a tie.
For not asking to take a nap,
For sitting too long with the cat on his lap.
For not making the bed her way,
For not tidying his books away.

Tessy Braun

Suzanne now has a new life.

She took the old one with a kitchen knife.
So if you have a partner
Who is kind and treats you well,
Yet is messy, which you *think* makes your life hell,
Then remember of this frightful tale I tell,
Because things could be a lot worse!

This poem illustrates my frustration over people that make a fuss of minor imperfections that their partners may have, this vex of mine is further explored on page 144.

Death By Cello

Her name was Ophelia Rose.
This was not the life that she chose.
She was a slave to a man that she loathed,
But from childhood they were betrothed.

She was ever so tragically beautiful,
And always exceptionally dutiful.
She'd always obey her master,
Who could've foreseen a disaster?

They lived in a fairy tale castle,
All the riffraff thought it divine!
Not in their wildest dreaming,
The set of a hideous crime...

The master was always so jealous,
Because she was a beautiful cellist.
The music she played he relished,
The melody he thoroughly cherished.

Though she was kind and obedient,
He was cunning and devious.
He was always acting so serious,
But her vibrato just made him delirious!

Ophelia Rose was up late at night
Playing her instrument by the moonlight,
Wondering how she would escape her plight,
And how maybe eventually she'd be alright.

The master was watching secretly,
Smiling to himself gleefully.
He approached from behind,
With a grisly plan in his mind.

He tore the bow from her hand,
The foulest and nastiest man!
In rage he threw the cello down,
The smash was heard across the town.

Tessy Braun

He pulled out the metal spike
And although she tried in vain to fight,
He used this awful musical weapon
And worked out all his rage and aggression!

She bled out from her wounds,
Sadly dying too soon.
But he only felt mellow
This ghastly old fellow!
And now she is dead,
In a *death caused by cello*.

No Regret

I dreamt of you last night.
Just a dream, yet it felt so true.
You pulled my hair so tight,
And smacked my face hard too.

> Yet next you were stroking my forehead,
> And rubbing my temples to soothe.
> So softly curled up in our bed,
> There's no other man I would choose!

> But then I awoke from this nightmare,
> Confused and in a cold sweat.
> I recalled you're now burning in hell,
> And in sending you I have *no regret!*

Tessy Braun

Time For A Change

He furiously threw his hands in the air
And shouted out in a raging despair.
"I give up now, and I no longer care!"
Though these outbursts were somewhat rare,
He would get mad, worked up,
And would shout, curse and swear.

His manager recapped his progression.
And said *"Despite your depression,*
While you've achieved in the past,
Performance never lasts;
You really must consistently improve".
Yet he stuck up his two fingers
With nothing to lose
And cried...

"I can't do the job, I don't need the stress!
I can't hit the grade, I've tried my darn best.
Despite what I do, I can't sell for you,
You're making me ill, you're making me blue!"

A laborious sigh, from the frustrated coach.
Having coached for some time,
There's no other approach!
You see, the skills he possesses
Yet he will not apply,
He doesn't achieve, you can ask yourself why.

So he trundled along feeling sorry for himself.
Feeling bitter and rejected
And concerned for his health.
He dragged his team down,
A truly miserable man,
Being monitored closely
With an improvement plan.

The moral of the story -
Aim to achieve and win!
In everything you do put 100% in.
Embrace guidance and advice you're sent

Open Book

(Don't take offence, as it's often well meant).
And if it *still* makes you so sad,
And if you still *always* feel bad,
If your targets *still* feel out of range...
Then maybe, just maybe
It's *time for a change*...

Tessy Braun

Bluebell Blanket

In the little woodland clearing
A *bluebell blanket* looks endearing.

Though be cautious as you stroll around,
Where flower fairies may be found,
Whispering their fairy talk
Peering passed the flower stalks.

But in the drooping recurved tips,
Inside a wandering child fits
And flower fairies lay their trap
With sticky sticky bluebell sap.
And once they've surely captured them
They drag that flower by the stem

Deep into the deathly dell,
They drag and drag that flower bell!
So be tempted not by their sweet scent
Or the beauty of that bluebell leant
And swaying in that gentle breeze,
For fairies take just as they please!

Mr Toad

I want to dance today with you
Across the lily pads.
You're such a graceful shiny frog,
It makes me rather sad
That you won't even look at me,
For I am ugly, so I'm told.
I'm warty and my skin is thick,
A silly croaking, *Mr Toad*!

I hear you 'ribbit' beautifully,
A pretty froggy croak,
But as I take a deep breath in
I start to cough and choke!
I spin around and tumble down,
Then flop into the pond.
I wish I could be graceful,
Can you wave a magic wand?

You laugh with glee at poor old me
As I wipe water from my eyes.
I'm such a clutz, it's all too much,
So it's time for my demise!
I clasp some grass, sharp as a knife,
And slice my skin to end my life.
And then I cry – "*I don't want to die!*"
But alas it's time say goodbye.

The moral of the story;
Don't get stuck in a rut,
And let anyone make you feel
Like you don't give a fuck.
You may feel downtrodden,
But let it not be forgotten
That you're a beautiful creature,
Despite your less beautiful features!

Tessy Braun

A Golden Potion

I crept into the forest - heard the groan of wild boar,
Nothing could prepare me for the sight that I saw.
There a frail old lady with her bones sticking out,
From her wrinkly body, two wings there did sprout!
She whispered a song "I am dying my dear,
Take this little blue bottle and please do not fear".

You will live forever, no more stormy weather

She then faded away into sparkling dream dust,
Her last weary words were "In God you must trust".
Her glittery ashes swirled round in a dance
And dived into the bottle, a potion of chance.
I swallowed the potion of shimmering gold,
For a promise of rebirth to stories once told.

The liquid it burned, as it slipped down my throat,
And a misty green vapour caused me to choke.
With a whizz and a bang and a sizzle and pop
I withered and wriggled to a time long forgot.
My silvery hair now turned to brunette,
My face became smooth with no lines of regret!
And to a dimension where time doesn't tick,
Where I'll never grow older - time's stopped for this
witch!

I will live forever, no more stormy weather

Down In A Hole

Down in a hole in a nest full of thorns,
A most hideous creature has been born.
It ruins lives; yet it has been said
That somebody loves its wicked ways.

It wants to please but wickedness stays.
It tries to do good but hate always remains.
The most wicked of creatures that ever did live,
With the emptiest heart and no love to give.

**Interestingly I found this writing scribbled down in
an old note book from my childhood. I did tweak it a
little but in the main it was my original writing.**

Tessy Braun

Selfie With A Camel

I took a *selfie with a camel*,
He didn't seem impressed,
The grumpy humpy mammal
Looked unquestionably distressed!

We posed for that selfie
To get the perfect pic,
But he didn't look that healthy,
And he spat some camel spit!

He snorted and he snuffled,
He didn't smell that great…
He seemed a little troubled
But then he started to gyrate!

It was then I heard the beat,
The Arab tunes, they flowed!
Then he got up on his feet,
And his yellow teeth he showed!

He boogied with his belly,
He stood on his hind feet,
I forgot he was so smelly,
As we danced to that beat!

So I was pleased as punch
With my happy camel friend!
And I kinda had a hunch,
That it would no longer offend…

So I got my camera out,
Called the obligatory "cheese"!
We both gave a selfie pout,
Before all over me he sneezed!

So I got my camel portrait,
But it really was quite vile.
Camel snot across my face,
But at least I got a smile!

Down The Bluebell Path

Down the bluebell path,
Violet-blue the way,
Whispering fairies dance
For revelation day!
Listen for their wings
That soft harmonic swish,
When Bluebell Fairies sing
It's time to make a wish!

Tessy Braun

Tawny Owl

I heard the hoot of a tawny owl,
Was it you, was it you?
I heard the mountain black bear growl,
Was it you, was it you?

I saw the moth still as could be,
Were you looking back at me?
I gazed at clouds and saw you there,
Smiling back without a care.

I heard the cuckoo sound it's coo,
It was you, it was you!
The kingfisher across the river flew,
A flash of green, a flash of blue.

The squirrel cracked its nut with care,
Was it you, were you there?
The little lamb that cried its bleat,
The swooshing of the bats wings beat.

You're all around, you're nature now,
That puma on his midnight prowl,
But something special happens when
I hear the hoot of the tawny owl!

Fiends In The Woods

Wild wolf howls
Under full moon.
Unearthly growls,
The witches croon.
Yelping, barking,
Savage cries.
Mantra chanting,
Watching eyes.
Forrest deeply
Full of beasties,
Supernatural
Interspecies!

Do you dare to step inside
And find out where these *fiends* do hide?

Tessy Braun

The Fox In The Snow

The fox in the snow
Stood by the stream
With ice on his coat,
He looked really mean.

He yelped to the night,
A cry that chilled bones,
On that wild winter night
The dark forest groaned.

The fox in the snow,
He looked right at me,
The spirit of the dead,
This lone fox could see.

April's Comb

He found among the seaweed on his evening wander home, a peculiar washed-up item inscribed with "*April's Comb*". It truly looked so pretty, a fisher's lucky find! An elegantly crafted comb, someone had left behind. The next day he wandered by the pebbled shore, and came across a purse abandoned by the ocean floor! For some time he pondered on where to keep his loot, but then he found the perfect spot that would so aptly suit.

He hung the treasure in the cab of his trawler boat with pride, and jingle-jangled in the sun the trophies side by side! One calm morning out at sea, he heard a mournful wail calling from the unknown depths, a sea sprite with a tail! She rose out of the water, her eyes a misty grey, holding out a salty limb, she gestured him her way. He couldn't understand her song, a language quite unheard. She held up her tangled hair and from this signal he inferred that there was something she had lost and longed to take back home. 'Twas the Mermaid, April, and he had found her comb!

She opened her palm to show two coins. and pointed to the trawler. For she had found her mermaid's purse there dangling over water. 'Twas then the fisher understood and handed her his hoard, she gave a smile and blew a kiss then tossed the coins on board! The fisher told his story of the mermaid that he saw, but none believed it could be true, therefore his story was ignored! But when out in the ocean, in those depths unknown, he hears that distant humming of sweet April with her comb!

Tessy Braun

Vita

Poetry inspired by living (And dying)

Tessy Braun

Glastonbury Dreamland

The wooden beads and metal mesh
Draped over my hand.
This is my memoir of the
Glastonbury dreamland.

The endless party,
Overlooking Egypt once again.
So why do I feel so much pain?

I wish I was back there among
All those happy, careless people.
All those colours in the dance tent -
Pink, yellow and purple.
I wish I was resting at the stone circle.

I danced and danced to Seb Fontaine.
I was in heaven again,
Playing this dangerous game.
And after our little rave
We floated over to the 'Other' stage.

What can I say? REM,
Really **E**motional **M**emory.
I couldn't keep my eyes off this famous band!

Sunday night was perfect at the end of the day
When someone took my breath away...

I know I was tired and longed for my bed,
But now I am home
An eerie reality hits me.

I don't want to work,
To answer the phone.
I don't want to go home!
My home was a canvas sheet
In a field in Avalon.

Tessy Braun

I was out in the open air
And the weather was fair.
And now I have showered
And washed my hair,
I feel clean – but I don't care.

I miss *Glastonbury*!

Glastonbury 2003 – My first – and last!

The Airport

The Airport a place of emotion,
Where sadness so oft can be seen,
The Airport - it's such a commotion,
Before boarding that flying machine!

The Airport, where reconciliation
Brings tears of pure happiness too,
The Airport the start of vacation
Opportunity waiting for you!

Vulcano

Today we're climbing a Volcano,
Such an awesome place to go!
Setting off on our adventure,
In sun screen head to toe.

It's so hot -we're going to die!
Yet we soldier on and we're getting really high.
We're treading through volcanic ash
All three of us melting with heat rash!

I said to my mummy "*I just can't do it*".
Exhaustion had kicked into my bones,
And I just wanted to go back home!

We're standing at the crater,
It's massive and vast!
We conquered the ascent,
"*More water please*!" I gasp.

Daddy stood right at the edge.
I was frightened he may fall!
We were so very tall,
Looking down at the village so small.

This was the day we climbed *Vulcano*.

I am so proud we made it!
Bravo! Bravo! BRAVO!

I wrote this piece on request of my (then) 9 year old niece, Alyss, who had just recently been on holiday to the Aeolian Islands. Hopefully this poem captures her arduous journey up 'Vulcano".

Monster

Anticipation, anxiety and fear,
A recipe for power
To feed the *Monster* looming near.

Maybe I'm small and perhaps
Some may think weak,
Yet in my soul lies an indestructible streak.

Hand me the *Monster* and I will perform,

He is the giant, but I am the storm!
I'll prove you were wrong
If you think I will fail,
Dancing in dirt for this sweet filthy tale.

p.s.

I'm trying to be brave,
I'm trying not to shudder
When I think of the obstacles
I'll face at *Tough Mudder*!

**I completed Tough Mudder in 2016, and it will not be
an experience that I will repeat EVER again!**

Christmas Eve

It's *Christmas Eve* and there's magic in the air,
I can feel excitement bubbling everywhere!

Little children love the sparkles and lights
And all the magic of the Christmas nights!

And all the love and cuddles Christmas brings,
Toys, sweets and chocolates, O what delightful things!

Here are my two boys Oliver and Joshua ready to go to school in their Christmas jumpers! They love Christmas and always look forward to the elves, Ben and Ivy coming to stay!

Christmas

Twinkling fairy lights
Entwined in Norway pine.
Gingerbread men smiling
For the love of *Christmas* time.

Little glass baubles shining
All around the room.
Excited little children hoping
Father *Christmas* will come soon.

The little elves will soon be here,
To join in with the *Christmas* cheer.

To see what mischief the kids may cause,
And report their findings to Santa Claus.

And as the advent doors are opened wide
Each day a tasty treat inside.
And *Christmas* Eve is here at last,

The children close their eyes
And fall asleep quite fast!

Then *Christmas* day for the little ones

Is one bundle of endless fun.
But us adults can *finally* relax...
Once the whole thing's all been done!

Tessy Braun

Shining Your Love

I feel so emotional
To see the room so bare.
When just a few hours earlier
You were *shining your love* just there.

Each precious hanging charm
Packed safe and snug away.
In a cardboard box up in the loft,
Until December comes again.

Ticking Clock

Another Christmas drawing near,
Soon to end another year.
The **ticking clock** never stops,
I dream of moments long forgot.

I don't forget my early life,
And I'd return in a blink of an eye.
Sweet memories of freedom and youth.
I'd go back in time, to tell you the truth...

A picture taken in a caravan at St Ives Bay Holiday Park in West Cornwall. A place where I take my two young boys now. I write a lot about the lovely places in Cornwall and other places in South West England. My collection "Travels with Tessy" is available on Amazon worldwide.

Fiery Ambition

Distance running sets me free,
Fiery ambition powering me.
Now halted by an injury
Alas, I feel a misery!

> I'll have to rest and do my stretches,
> Massage, ice so healing progresses.
> But in the end will I cry or laugh,
> Will I complete the Cardiff Half?

In 2016 I became massively into running. I didn't let having a three year old get in my way as you can see in this image. I used to go out running with the pushchair and it was no mean feat!

Thirteen Miles

Part of a wave in a sea of thousands,
The anticipation and excitement is fizzing
As though in a glass and spilling over,
As we wait in our starting pen.
Not six, not seven, nor nine, neither ten,
But *thirteen miles* to run,
And eagerly awaiting the sound of the gun!

I am injured, and never had I thought
(Even by taking the painkillers that I'd brought)
That I would run up to nine miles
Without needing to walk!

Only momentarily to start with.
A bit of a walk, a bit of a run.
By mile ten it wasn't feeling as fun
And was more than just a niggle...

I marched along and jogged small amounts
When I felt I could try.
And though try as I might, it didn't feel right.

With one mile to go the end was in sight.
I managed to slowly and gently persevere
Inspired by the crowd's supportive cheer.

My medal proudly around my neck.
But I didn't beat my personal best.
Though at two hours thirty six minutes.
I'm still fairly impressed.
So well done me!
(But now it's time to rest my knee!)

I did indeed complete the Cardiff half Marathon on 1st October 2017. As the poem explains it was not without a considerable amount of pain!

Tessy Braun

Accept His Imperfections

I don't mean to present any offence,
But sometimes it's not easy
To keep up the pretense.
As I scroll through your premium lifestyle,
It really grates on me, reading through your profile.
I guess I'm only full of envy,
The list could be quite lengthy
To compete with your perceived excellency.
I'd be grateful, not hateful
For the things you possess.
I think you're lucky, not mucky
Your solution's no mess!
There's no 'real' pollution
So why are you distressed?

Don't you have it all? Aren't you the fool?
Because what I would give, if I could live
In a stable way, not struggling every day.
But you, you quibble about such minor situations.
You're not abused, you're not used,
Nor have turbulent relations
Or jealous accusations
So why feel these frustrations?

Accept his is slothful, not awful.
Sometimes needs a push
To be reminded, he's not as high minded
As you seem to be.
But his kindness is something
I'm not blinded to see,
Even if he doesn't pack the bags perfectly,
Or always have a sense of urgency.

Ophelia

The sky Halloween orange,
The sun a ruby red.
A sign from the heavens,
Our ancestors would have said.

The whistling wind picks up speed
And at its mercy the flowers plead.
The charm jangling a melodic tune.
The atmosphere is eerie,
A storm is coming soon.

Nature is moving out of sync,
Taken over by some wild instinct.
The world transforms to a creepy place,
Wildlife seeks refuge now in haste.
Ophelia is coming and there's no time to waste.

Hurricane Ophelia battered the British isles in September 2017 with wind speeds up to 185km/hr I remember shortly before her arrival coming out of the supermarket and absorbing the eerie atmosphere that had developed while I had been in the store. It was a most strange ambience, and gave me inspiration to capture this natural phenomenon caused by the impending storm.

Tessy Braun

Weep

I can't sleep for I just *weep*.
But in time my dreams I meet.

I wake, and for a second feel
Refreshed until I know it's real.

I breathe deep and once more *weep*.
For this nightmare is here to keep.

Here is a picture of my mum and dad (Gerhard and Rosemary) with my sister (Gabriella) and me as a tiny baby. This poem was written when I found out that my dad had terminal cancer. I wanted to share with you this lovely photo of us all together so many years ago (1982).

Isolation Room

I clutch my aching stomach tight
With nausea creeping day and night.
Additionally I've caught the flu.
There's nothing that the docs can do.

Lonely are these four white walls.
Isolated with no talk at all.
In this clinical room I lie,
Thinking *I don't want to die*!

The few that come will wear a mask,
Gloves and apron too they're asked.
Feels like the nurse forgot of me,
I'm left alone despairingly!

Hour pass, then days as well
Merge into one long stretch of hell!
Why me? How did I deserve?
This cancer really has a nerve!

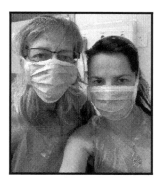

My sister and I were instructed to wear these masks when visiting dad in hospital to prevent the potential spread of flu to other patients. This photo haunts me, yet also depicts a touch of black humour!

Tessy Braun

Death

Death

Cruel and uncompromising you are.
Swooping like a claw,
Snatching at our flesh and bones.
Draining colour from our rosy tones.

To dust we crumble,
To the earth we return.
To rot in the ground or ferociously burn.
Here, facing life's vicious brutality,
I am reminded of my own mortality.

Life's Circle

I wish I had known you both better,
Though my memories are just a mere haze.
And mixed with the tales I've heard re-told
Of years gone by in the 'good old days'.

But grandma, I only have photos,
Only pictures of moments in time.
And Grandad I can barely remember
A time when your arms wrapped around mine.

So life's ever turning *circle* spins,

My mum and dad now grandparents too.
Now I fear for the circle still turning
And that one day I'll also lose you.

A short time after I wrote this piece our family had the devastating news that my father Gerhard was diagnosed with inoperable stomach cancer.

Picture above is my grandparents, Irene and Percy Adams with my sister Gabriella.

Tessy Braun

Dad's Poem

December comes, then Christmas time
Glasses raised and time to dine,
One last time, one last time.
But we didn't get our "one last time".

Ways to remember you
There's so much to say!
Head chef of the Holiday Inn
(Back in those good old days).
For royals and celebs, food you prepared,
Not forgetting politicians like Tony Blair.
And how lovely that Tammy
Sent you her book,
With her message of love
And of how skilfully you cooked.

More ways ..

Little straw stars and German Christmas cookies,
Your homemade nativity all mossy and woody.
A fine glass of wine or Bavarian beer,
Oh daddy, oh daddy,
I wish you were here.

It wasn't always easy
But you were a hardworking man.
You achieved, and we're so proud of you,
The master of the ship you ran!

Dartmoor was your special place
And many times with you
We walked across the moors
To enjoy that timeless view.

Letterboxing years ago
Adventures you would seek,
A game of chess, modern art
And love for your antiques.

Open Book

St Ives in West Cornwall,
camping at Lower Treave,
Trips to the Isles of Scilly,
You loved the roaring sea.

And all around your home were
Little trinkets of your trips,
Exploring this big world of ours
In your retirement bliss.
Visiting places in the sun
Jet setting and a'cruising -
New York just *had* to be done!

But life's cruel fate came knocking
And took you from our reach,
The disease there was no stopping
For a cure we do beseech.

No more corridors or shiny floors,
Door's swinging hinges, ticking clocks
Or filled syringes.

Daddy, you are now at peace,
Daddy, you can sleep at ease
No more pain, no more pain.

Farewell until we meet again.

In the weeks leading up to dad leaving us, he asked me to write a poem about him to read at his funeral. Thank you to Shelley Cooper who helped me with the penultimate stanza.

145

Tessy Braun

Selfish

I hatched a plan to implement
To learn another instrument.
So I tucked a violin
Underneath my eager chin.

And as I began to play
My sad sister could only say
"You took my instrument away,
You play the cello anyway!"

Additionally family members have implied,
That I'm **selfish** to act upon my heart or mind.

It seems I've only one role to fulfil,
Though if I'm only mum, I think I'll fall ill!

For in our family I'm mum *and* dad,
Life's so stressful and I'm often sad.
So creativity makes me feel less mad,
So ***please***, don't make me feel so bad!

The Young Ones

Intoxicated and getting wasted.
Vodka shots rolls down my tongue.
Partying hard like I did once,
In the years when I was young.

The young ones drink down shot after shot.
Smoke cigarettes (and I'm sure I smell pot).
It's alright for them - tomorrow they can rot,
Their tiredness and headaches will soon be forgot.

But my boys will wake at five in the morning,
Spritely and loud and without prior warning!
I had a great night, it was fun and exciting,
But tonight I'm looking forward to
Just chilling and writing.

Choices

How do you know the best route to take?
How might you come to your *choice*?

How can you tell what decision to make?
Do you wait for wisdom or some inner voice?

How do you not make the same mistake twice?
Is it just chance, like the roll of the dice?

No...

Think with your mind and don't be lead
By the butterflies enchanting your head.
No, don't be flighty and foolish
By thinking with your heart.
To achieve the very best outcome
You must try to be smart!

So I Write

I wrestle with a somber fear,
And lately it strikes me so often.
How in one's life, memories
Become lost or perhaps just forgotten.

Think how quickly we lose a day,
A week, and each passing year.
Time dwindles away so quickly,
These precious moments disappear.

Never to see them again, gone for all of time,
Slowly slipping away with each tick tock chime.
Left at the least as mixed up thoughts
Jumbled up and intertwined.

Locked away in the attic of the world,
So much of your life may remain untold.
Friendships and lovers that no longer last,
Secrets and memories locked in the past.

So I journal,
So I write.
To keep my stories wrapped up tight.

Tessy Braun

Carefree Times

I close my tired and weary eyes
And re-live those fun
And *carefree times*.

Those days that were
Full to the brim,
With freedom, choice and
spontaneity and sin.

Fridays after work
We would head to the bars.
We could dance all night
And reach for the stars!

We'd feel bloody awful
The following day
(But no children to wake us
for a six am play!)

We'd follow the band on a Saturday
night.
We'd be dance at the front with all of our might.
We would really enjoy the show,
Me and my sister at Bazooka Joe!

Now we have a different lifestyle,
But I still miss the old one
(*Just once in a while*).

Book Dreaming

I truly miss getting lost in a *book*,
There's a pile collecting dust on my table.
I often plan to snuggle down and read,
But it's rare nowadays that I ever succeed.

There's always something else on my list
That gets a priority over this.
I do wish I could turn my chores away
And tidy the house another day.

By the time I am cosy and turning a page
My eyes are beginning to close.
My tired head tells me it's time to sleep
And my *book* falls flat on my nose!

Demons

I crudely let my *demons* out,

Furiously I scream and shout.
Obscenities are thrown about,
You've hit a nerve without a doubt.

Superior you claim to be.
"Genius" supremacy.
(Impetuous insanity?).
But will you show me clemency?

Garden Song

When I glance out at my *garden*
I feel a wave of pride!
Yes I know it 'aint no Chelsea,
But it makes me warm inside!

I transformed my garden all alone
(Though some would think I lied).
I threw anxiety on its back,
And forced myself outside.

So now rescued from a sorry state,
My garden has a different fate.
Now horsetails won't submerge its beauty
And flowers bloom in royal duty!

Tessy Braun

Don't Say You Love Me

Don't say you love me
Just for attention.
Don't walk behind me
In search of a mention.

Shower me only with true love and affection,
If you don't like my thinking,
Then please change direction!

Don't say you love me,
For your own selfish needs,
Don't say I'm wonderful,
If you do not agree.

Pour over me only your genuine praise,
If you want, offer guidance
Please don't be afraid!

Sure, tell me your thoughts -
Be respectful and kind,
This way you can help me
And new skills I may find.

But don't say you love me,
Just for attention.
Don't walk behind me
In search of a mention.

A Friend In You

I am so incredibly proud,
So I want to shout out loud,
That in you what a wonderful *friend* I've found!

Thank you for tolerating my laborious ways,
And for being by my side throughout messy days.

Oh what a year it's been,
Such a lot has transpired.
I'm so glad you were inspired
By my 'detective style'
Because now your family has grown in size,
And you've got an amazing reason to smile!
And maybe, by the end of the year
You'll take the next step.
(Reunite with your mother,
But I know it's complex).
And your little sister too.
I know how much you miss her.

This year will be the year for you.
You've put on and tied up your running shoes,
Baby steps but you'll get there eventually.
Stay motivated and you'll get there successfully!

We've had so much fun this year.
Historic houses, carveries and giraffes,
Our initial trip to Bath.
Lots of messages
And plenty of laughs,
And written paragraphs.
And we've watched fabulous TV!
Tudors, and not forgetting Line of Duty, my **DC**!

For Billy x

Tessy Braun

Change In The Air

Giddy with summer and still feeling high,
When the stifling heat has kissed us goodbye.

This *change in the air* gives me tingles of zest
For love of the season I long for the best.

Hallow's Eve, bonfires and birthdays galore,
And next we find Yuletide festivities in store!

Perpetual Motion

Life spins around in *perpetual motion*,
A endless journey of mixed emotions.
Billions of years preceded you and me,
But will life keep going for eternity?
Or one day will there be an end to this place?
Will they send us up to outer space?
What will become of our human race?

Tessy Braun

Small Pathetic Lives

How insignificant we truly are.
Going about our busy little lives
On this tiny patch of planet Earth.
Just one tiny fraction of the universe.

We're but nothing,
Just tiny drops of rain.
Here for just a miniscule of time.
Then back into the earth where we remain.

We're not a chapter, we're not even a book.
We're just one of trillions of animals
Crawling on the planet's surface,
Trying to find a purpose
In our *small pathetic lives*.

Lost In Time

Lost in time, lost in space,
This species called the human race.
Life is a curious thing,
Searching for meaning in everything.
And swarming on earth's surface,
Pondering over our very purpose.
Spinning at galactic pace,
Lost in time and lost in space.

We're made from stardust
If in science you trust.
Our feelings include our hatred
Passion, guilt and lust.
Or is there more to our story
Of the human race and territory?
Who knows the secret of life itself,
In this global laboratory!

Lost in time, lost in space,
Perhaps one day the end we'll face,
The ending of our planet blue,
The end of life on earth for you.
And will they beam us up to Mars,
Passing by the moon and stars,
To a new home in the milky way;
Will life go on? We hope and pray.

Tessy Braun

Fiesta

Summer's begun and don't we know it.
Love's in the air and we all show it.
Music, chanting, drumming, dancing,
Fiesta days, summer romancing!

Sun's burning, memories blurring,
Wine is flowing, skin is glowing.
Costumes and flirtatious feathers,
Hot air balloons and fun endeavors!

Tie dyed clothes on make shift rails,
Mermaids with their scaled tails,
Carnival has come to town,
Nothing's gonna bring me down!

Live Today

Live today and think not of tomorrow.
Fear not what life may
Or may not bring you.
And worry not.
Take just today and be happy.

Be thankful
For the precious things you have.
Long not for more.

For what will be will be.

Tessy Braun

Abbie

Abbie, you were so sweet.

Being your owner was such a treat.
You were a creature gentle all round,
With pretty markings of white and brown.

You were never nippy or skittish,
You found dried corn snacks delicious.
You'd circle around on your flying dish,
But climbing and swinging was your true wish.

Now you've closed your eyes to sleep,
And peacefully resting, forever you keep,
Abbie, you were our perfect pet,
A sweet hamster we will never forget.

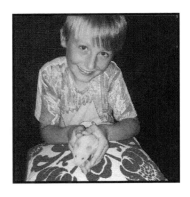

A Silver Gift Bag

When I'm watching television,
Like Luther or Les Miserables,
I often glance over at the cabinet
And catch a glimpse of your picture.
With your tall chef's hat
Holding that fish out on a silver plate.

Then I remember that your kind face
Is no longer warm or soft to touch,
Your body is no longer in the form
That I see in the image,
But now just a pile of bone ash,
A glance away,
In a green plastic jar,
In a *silver gift bag*.

Tessy Braun

Honey

No, I did not buy the *honey*,

Condemning me, condemning me.
Stripped the bed to try to help,
Was not worth the anguish felt.
Sisters under so much stress
Trying to do what is best,
No, I did not buy the *honey*,

Condemning me, condemning me.

Rainbow

That *rainbow* on the M5
It's arch from end to end,
It made me feel alive,
Colours bright across its bend.

The magic of that rainbow,
Its sight evoked in me,
A reflection of its beauty
That one day I'll no longer see.

For you that day is closer,
This world you'll soon depart.
How quick a life is lived,
From first beating of a heart.

And when you've slipped away,
If a rainbow's in my view,
I'll think of you dear father,
And all the love I have for you.

Tessy Braun

If

If the doctor had taken more care,
I can't help but think you'd still be there.
Indigestion, that only got worse,
If only you'd told us your symptoms at first.

I can't help but feeling in so many ways
That with closer attention you could've been saved.
If you had gone back, like the doctor had said

I really don't think that today you'd be dead.
If you hadn't come down with the flu that day

There wouldn't have been such a delay
With the laparoscopy going ahead,
And maybe the cancer wouldn't have spread.

**"Ifs" and "Buts" won't bring him back, but
sometimes I can't help but thinking things could
have been different.**

They Weep

On that familiar road,
A dusky light does creep,
And all along the horizon
The granite tors *they weep*.

The landscape falls and rises,
In sombre mood she moans.
The sad songs of the moorland
Echo through her bones.

The silhouettes they haunt us -
St Michaels on Brent Tor.
Our sleeping lion of Sheepstor
Lets out a desperate roar.

A twilight murk fills the air,
Heaviness now hangs low.
I beg the moor to stop her tears,
Not let her sadness show.

Along that stretch of road
The edge of Dartmoor sweeps,
And all along the horizon,
The granite tors they weep.

Tessy Braun

My Daddy's Dead

I saw you face the end of life,
If you can do it, so can I.
It's said that once you've seen blood drain
That nothing is the same again.
To see you take one final breath,
Then begin your venture into death
Was really quite a privilege,
To be there when away you slid.
But as you left you looked in fear,
I hope you knew that we were near.
We'll never know what thoughts you had
Or if your death was good or bad.

And there you lay all stiff and white,
Your eyes widened in a fright.
Your jaw locked open, skin turned cold,
An awful image to behold.
I stroke your cheek, you're cold like ice,
My daddy's dead, it isn't nice.
I touch your skin to comprehend,
It's over now, this is the end.
I saw you face the end of life,
If you can do it, so can I.
It's said that once you've seen blood drain
That nothing is the same again.

My Dad In A Box

Snug in your coffin,
Waxy and neat,
My dad in a box
For a last winter's sleep.

A light summer jacket,
Purple socks on your feet.
A blue pin striped shirt,
I sit there and weep.

Embalmed and preserved -
For what and for why?
They drained out your blood
For a daughters goodbye.

You were certainly peaceful,
But you weren't quite the same,
Your lips were too full,
Your face had been changed.

I had read all about it,
The embalmers tools,
How they plump up the flesh
With cotton wool balls.

How they stitch up the eyes,
How they make up the face.
Try to make them life like,
For the poor viewer's sake.

Your hands were like ice
Your body so bony,
I capture an image
Of you dead and lonely.

My dad in a box,
I touch his cold hand,
I take one last glance
Before turning around.

169

Tessy Braun

A Journey

I could not face
The lonely A30.
The Highwayman Inn
Reminds me
Too much of him.
So instead
A ski slope
And a row of
White sails of hope
Welcome me home,
To my ocean city.
Past Argyle,
The Jack Rabbit,
And dad's old flat.
But then signs
To that monstrosity
Of a hospital
With its tall chimney
Haunt me,
And I remember
Those brave
But ghastly trips,
And those
Answers we
Didn't want to hear.
Signs to Tavi,
More memories
O they trap me!
Realisation sets in
That never will
This place
Be the same.
A journey cursed
With thoughts of a man,
My father,
Living and breathing
In a road,
In a city,
A town,
A journey

School Playground

I've never been the '*school playground*' kind of mum,
Cliques and huddles make me turn and run!
Not to say I'm not friendly with some,
I just don't fit in with those "*popular*" mums.

All that banter and snide sneering that you hear
Makes me uncomfortable as I stand near.
I say, don't judge - you don't know the full picture,
Some children don't fit in with your parenting scripture.

No, I don't hang around in the school grounds,
I'd rather quickly flee from those gossiping crowds,
Because for those who have their tuppence to say,
I don't care for your prattle and meddling today!

Tessy Braun

Wicked Dreams

Excitement is bubbling inside of me,
The anticipation churns over delightfully.
We're in the front row stalls tonight,
Eyes level with the stage, such a delight!

Not just once or twice have we been,
But *nine* times to see the witch of green!

We're quite the experts my sister and I,
Dancing through life we 'Re-joicify!'.

The costumes so wonderfully splendid,
Lavish and colourful, and I often pretended
That I was the actress - the star of the show,
To travel by bubble, I should like to go!

To the stage, the music, the lights and fame,
The theatre audience will call out my name!
And then when it's time for the curtain call,
I stride out with a smile and wave out to all.

But plummeting down to a pitiful reality.
Back to my seat, I'm just a mere wannabe...
Dreaming big and imagining splendour,
But on Monday I'm back in the freaking call centre!

Birthing Partner

You sat in the bath
Having a laugh,
Occupying yourself
So the time went fast.

I was groaning in labour
But you did me no favour,
Like rubbing my back
(Your affection did lack).

And when he was born,
Your mood was forlorn,
Like the end of your life
At this new break of dawn.

And then before long
You made sure we were gone,
With your family so fierce
And your actions so wrong.

And many a time
You were very unkind
But I made my escape
And left you behind.

Yet I'll never forget
The time that I wept
As you lay in the bath
Having a laugh.

**Thankfully the birth of my second child was perfect
and I cannot fault my birthing partner one bit!**

Tessy Braun

Oh Daddy

Oh Daddy, I remember a time when I was small,
It doesn't seem that long ago, not long ago at all.
And Daddy, I remember all the moments we shared,
The beach, the moorland, and meals that you prepared.

Daddy I think fondly of days on Plymouth hoe,
The barbican, the bobbing boats,
Our favourite place to go!

I smile when I think about your place on Tavi road,
And how I used to stay with you,
Your love for me it showed.

Oh dad, I won't forget how you fetched me from the club.
I threw up out the window,
And you didn't thank me much.

And dad, I recall the words you penned
In those handwritten notes,
And all those times you rescued me
With all the cheques you wrote.

Now you have two grandsons
who love you with all their hearts.
You worked hard, and saved for them
To have a prosperous start.

Be brave Daddy, now you're near the end,
We're all so very frightened
And no longer can we pretend
That everything will be okay,
Or that this beast will go away.

Oh Daddy, you can rely on me,
When you need me I'll be there,
And every day there'll be a call
To show you that I care.

I Don't Care

Sometimes I'm in the kind of mood
To say whatever I like.
I think seriously, fuck you,
Because what you say is shite!

I put my "*I don't care*" defenses up"
And shoot my arrows fast.
And I don't care what you think of me -
I really can't be assed!

You didn't like my poem?
I'm sorry you feel that way.
I hope it get some likes,
'Cuz I'm gonna post it anyway!

There was a time when I may have been criticized for posting poems on Instagram that were too revealing or too true to my own personal feelings. I wrote this piece as a response to the person who disapproved! I thought this was a fierce and fiery piece to complete *Open Book***, I hope you enjoyed it!**

Tessy Braun

About The Author

Tessy is a mother of two lively young boys and enjoys an active life style with them. While originally from West Devon, Tessy now lives in Bristol, in the United Kingdom.

In addition to writing Tessy enjoys exploring the countryside and playing the violin and the cello. Tessy has been writing poetry and stories throughout her whole life but has only been publishing her work since 2018.

In *Open Book* Tessy has brought to you emotional poetry from the heart. Tessy also writes poetry about places in the South West of England. Her book **"Travels with Tessy"** showcases the delights of Devon, Cornwall and beyond through poetry and is available on Amazon worldwide. Other titles include:

"For None Would Hear"
A narrative poem exploring the tragic consequences of domestic abuse
"The Voice Of Six Tudor Queens"
Six historically accurate poems written from the viewpoint of Henry VIII's six wives

Tessy welcomes honest feedback and would be very grateful if you would take a moment to leave an honest review of *Open Book* on Amazon